Essential Lives

Alexander the Great

Essential Lives

ALEXANDER THE GREAT

ANCIENT KING & CONQUEROR

by **Katie Marsico**

Content Consultant:
D. Felton, Associate Professor of Classics
University of Massachusetts Amherst

ABDO
Publishing Company

CREDITS

Published by ABDO Publishing Company, 8000 West 78th Street, Edina, Minnesota 55439. Copyright © 2009 by Abdo Consulting Group, Inc. International copyrights reserved in all countries. No part of this book may be reproduced in any form without written permission from the publisher. The Essential Library™ is a trademark and logo of ABDO Publishing Company.

Printed in the United States.

Editor: Nadia Higgins
Copy Editor: Paula Lewis
Interior Design and Production: Nicole Brecke
Cover Design: Nicole Brecke

Library of Congress Cataloging-in-Publication Data
Marsico, Katie, 1980-
   Alexander the Great : ancient king & conqueror / by Katie Marsico.
      p. cm. — (Essential lives)
   Includes bibliographical references and index.
   ISBN 978-1-60453-520-4
   1. Alexander, the Great, 356-323 B.C.—Juvenile literature.
2. Greece—History—Macedonian Expansion, 359-323 B.C.—
Juvenile literature. 3. Greece—Kings and rulers—Biography—
Juvenile literature. 4. Generals—Greece—Biography—Juvenile
literature. I. Title.

DF234.M275 2009
938'.07092—dc22
[B]

                              2008033489

TABLE OF CONTENTS

Alexander the Great is depicted on Greek drachmas currency. Drachmas were used in Greece until the introduction of the euro in 2002.

A Horseman's Skills
and a Hint at Greatness

*P*rince Alexander studied the wild stallion with a determined stare, despite the fierce sun that beat down upon the countryside. It was summer in Macedonia, a kingdom directly north of ancient Greece. The prince was just 12 or so.

Nonetheless, young Alexander grasped the value of a strong yet obedient horse. His father, King Philip II, needed such a horse to rely on during battle.

The royal family had been observing the steed in a nearby field. The beast was physically impressive—but willful, too. Neither Philip nor any of his attendants could mount it. Now the furious king was shouting for the horse dealer to take the animal out of his sight.

Just as the horse was being led away, Alexander spoke up. He urged Philip to buy the stallion for him. The prince insisted that—although more practiced horsemen had attempted and failed—he would succeed in riding the animal. The king could not decide what to do. Should he scold his son for his boastful ignorance? Or should he laugh at the thought of such an inexperienced boy taming the wild creature? In the end, Philip allowed Alexander to try. However, the prince was to repay his father the full cost of the horse if he failed.

As Alexander confidently made his way toward the horse, the animal reared up. From a distance, Philip looked on with an anxious crowd. Would the prince be punished for his foolish arrogance with a fatal kick? The perceptive youth had a crucial, saving insight. He understood the reason for the creature's wild behavior. The stallion was frightened of his own shadow.

Alexander petted the nervous steed he was to name Bucephalas. He spoke in a calm, soothing voice. Then Alexander turned the horse to face the sun. Once the shadow was behind the stallion, the prince was able to gain greater control of the reins. Soon the pair was astounding spectators with Alexander's clever horsemanship and Bucephalas's speed and agility. A long-lasting partnership was formed that day. Alexander would continue to ride his beloved charger long after he was more than just a boy with unspoken dreams and unproven talent.

Perhaps just as important, however, were the words that Philip proclaimed after witnessing his son's impressive display. "My boy, you must find a kingdom big enough

"Ox Head"

The Greek name *Bucephalas* translates to "ox head."[1] If Alexander picked his stallion's name, as many experts suspect he did, there are a few possible explanations for his choice. Several historians believe that the animal had a white mark on its head that was in the shape of an ox. Others argue that the name may have been related to the horse's stubborn personality. Either way, the name Bucephalas echoes alongside Alexander's in historical accounts.

for your ambitions," he advised. "[Macedonia] is too small for you."[2] Few of those present could have guessed how amazingly accurate Philip's promise would ultimately prove.

COMMANDER, KING, AND CONQUEROR

Alexander III was born in Macedonia in 356 BCE. By the time he was 18, his father had conquered Greece. The mighty Greek empire was known for its cultural achievements and advanced political workings. Alexander lived

Reconstructing the Life of a Conqueror

How do modern historians know about Alexander's life? Artifacts such as weapons, jewelry, coins, and statues that date to that period in Greek civilization lend some clues about his existence.

In addition, ancient biographers including Arrian, Plutarch, and Quintus Curtius Rufus recorded detailed accounts of his campaigns and battles. However, as these writers were all born hundreds of years after Alexander's reign, they admitted that their work was probably flawed. They were also faced with the difficult task of recording a life that was brimming over with conquests and accomplishments. As Plutarch notes in his biography,

> The multitude of [his] great actions affords so large a field that I . . . forewarn my reader that I have chosen . . . the most celebrated parts of [his] story, [rather] than to insist at large on every particular circumstance of it.[3]

Today, scholars continue to piece together both written and archaeological clues to present Alexander's life as accurately and in as much detail as possible. In learning about the Macedonian ruler, they also gain valuable information about the numerous world cultures he influenced.

Exceptional Beings

Alexander so adored Bucephalas that he founded a city in his honor. The city Bucephala was where the horse died in approximately 325 BCE. Many historians believe Bucephala once existed in the area that is currently Jhelum, Pakistan. Alexander's action comes as no surprise, as he considered Bucephalas and his other horses to be far more than mere animals. From his perspective, the creatures were gifts from the gods.

amidst great power—as well as the violence and brutal competition that came with it. Leaders battled for control across the globe, within Greece, and even inside Alexander's own royal family. In the midst of these struggles, Alexander expressed the same bold confidence he had demonstrated with Bucephalas. He was intent upon achieving a greatness that other rulers had only dared to imagine. He refused to let anyone—either enemy kings or his own kinsmen—stop him.

Alexander became king of Macedonia at age 20. The young ruler wasted no time in pursuing his vision. He immediately set off to overtake the vast Persian empire, which included large portions of Asia and Africa. As he put his plans into action, he impressed his own troops as well as those of the enemy. The men marveled at Alexander's military genius and his passionate persistence.

However, his peers—as well as the numerous people he conquered—did not always understand

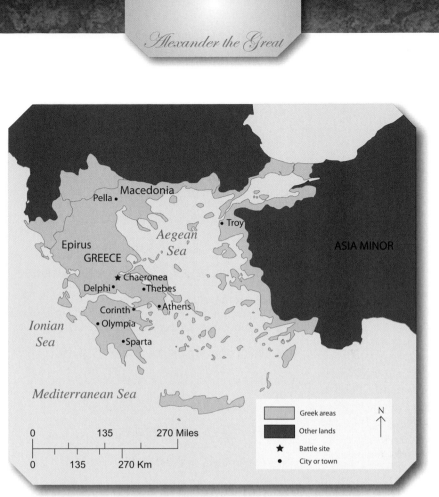

Alexander hailed from Macedonia. The kingdom combined with Greek city-states to form the ancient Greek empire when he was a teenager.

Alexander's ferocious appetite for world domination. He could be mercilessly cruel to his dearest friends and yet overwhelmingly compassionate to defeated foes. Whereas he enriched Greece and added to its glory, he also admired other cultures—occasionally too much so in the eyes of his countrymen.

On the Heels of Greatness

Philip was clearly proud of his son. But the two were known to share a strained and sometimes even competitive relationship. Philip would never control the expansive empire that Alexander ultimately created. However, he was a powerful ruler and fearless conqueror in his own right. Despite conflicts with his father, the young prince recognized the significance of Philip's accomplishments. As Alexander once remarked to his friends, "Boys, my father will forestall me in everything. There will be nothing great or spectacular for you and me to show the world."[4]

Alexander created a more extensive empire than anyone who preceded him and countless others who followed. He mingled his heritage with those of other civilizations. This resulted in a period of widespread Greek influence known as the Hellenistic era.

By age 32, Alexander the Great relished the thought of additional conquests in Asia and possibly even Africa and Europe. He died too soon to realize his final ambitions. Nonetheless, his legacy lives on in both history books and present-day cultures around the world. The boy who unlocked the secret to riding Bucephalas ultimately possessed the ability to rule much of the world. And the world would never be the same for it.

A live actor on a sculpted horse portrays Alexander during the opening ceremony of the 2004 Olympic Games in Athens, Greece.

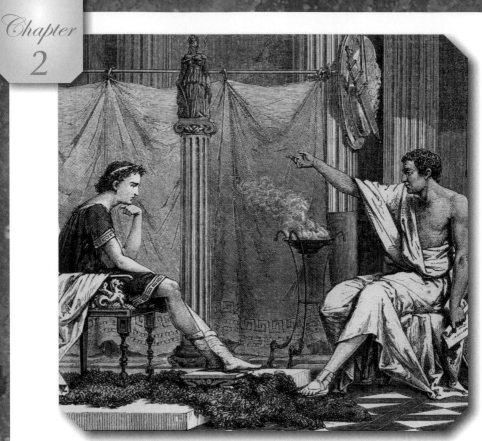

Chapter 2

The great Greek thinker Aristotle (right) served as Alexander's tutor.

RAISED TO RULE AN EMPIRE

E ven before Alexander was born, it appears the world believed he was destined for greatness. Both Philip and his wife, Queen Olympias, had experienced dreams rich with symbolic significance. Soothsayers interpreted their dreams to mean Olympias would one day bear a "bold and lion-like" son.[1] The queen gave birth in July 356 BCE, and Alexander innocently entered a life where he would indeed need those qualities to survive and excel.

Macedonia was not yet part of the Greek empire. During this time, Greece was made up of several independent, self-governing regions known as city-states. The city-states were constantly warring among themselves. Many of their leaders were eager to expand their lands and riches. Few, however, could match the Macedonian king's advanced army, strategic skills, or knack for getting exactly what he wanted.

To the dismay of the city-states, Philip had an appetite for domination that grew well beyond his kingdom's borders. Additionally, several city-states, including Athens and Thebes, bristled at the idea of a Macedonian ruler. Macedonians primarily dwelled in an area that is now divided between the Republic of Macedonia, Greece, and Bulgaria. Many Greeks considered Macedonians foreigners who did not share their heritage.

Philip's subjects did speak Greek. But they had a slightly different dialect compared to residents of the city-states. Also, their governments were strikingly different. Athens and other city-states generally elected their leaders. Or, at the very least, they allowed citizens to have a voice in political affairs. By contrast, Macedonia was controlled by kings who maintained power by whatever means necessary. These kings were known to resolve conflicts through warfare rather than words.

Such methods appeared harsh to some, but others argued they were necessary. Greece faced many foreign enemies who posed a threat. To the east, the immense Persian empire stretched from the Danube River in present-day Eastern Europe to the Indus River in the Indian subcontinent. The Persians had attacked the Greeks in 490 BCE and returned a decade later, setting fire to Athens. This inflamed a Greek desire for revenge that still burned bright at the time of Alexander's birth more than 130 years later.

Eager to See a Son Succeed

As heir to the Macedonian throne, Alexander was expected to be courageous and cunning in a society filled with conflict. Even palace life experienced plots and frequent bitter quarrels. Though Philip and Olympias had high hopes for their son, the king had at least five other wives, and perhaps as many as eight. He and Alexander's mother sometimes held opposing views, but the queen could hold her own in any argument. She was a political figure who was ruthlessly devoted to her son's future. She used her strong will and formidable intelligence to pursue Alexander's interests as she viewed them.

Olympias's motives did not stem just from motherly instinct. She also had a practical, personal reason for urging Alexander on. Philip's other wives could produce competing heirs. By cultivating her son's strength and self-confidence, Olympias essentially protected her and her children's wealth, status, and physical safety. If Alexander proved powerful enough to hold the throne, they were less vulnerable to attack.

From Philip's perspective, it was equally important to raise a child who could meet both the

Philip's Wives

The custom of taking more than one wife was not uncommon in Philip's culture. Most historians claim Philip had seven wives, but the Macedonian king may have had as many as eight. Either way, the marriages were a way for Philip to create alliances with nearby territories.

Olympias came from the kingdom of Epirus. She married Philip in approximately 357 BCE. Olympias appears to have been one of the few wives to produce for Philip a male heir. Though he had additional sons, one was mentally handicapped. Another was murdered while still an infant. Philip and Olympias also had a daughter named Cleopatra, who likely was born a year or two after Alexander.

physical and mental demands of the crown. The king required an intelligent, capable prince to ensure that his bloodline would be carried into future generations. Consequently, Philip was determined to see the boy brought up under the careful eye of Greece's most renowned teachers and trainers.

Despite the royal parents' differences of opinion, both recognized that it was in their best interests—as well as their son's—to raise a shrewd thinker, a skilled warrior, and a godlike leader.

Teachers and Training

Alexander lived in sumptuous surroundings at the palace in Pella, the capital city. Nevertheless, he was not allowed to daydream or waste his time on boyish games. As a prince, he received the finest education, including instruction from the famous Greek philosopher Aristotle. Alexander was tutored alongside the sons of other Macedonian nobles in a grove, or garden, in the nearby

His Favorite Book

Alexander so loved the *Iliad* that he later carried a copy of the epic poem with him during his travels and military campaigns. Historians believe he slept with the text—along with his sword—under his pillow at night. Perhaps, as Plutarch suggests, "[Alexander] regarded the *Iliad* as a handbook of the art of war."[2] Tales of Achilles' heroic exploits may have offered inspiration during Alexander's conquest of the Persian empire. Or the book may simply have reminded him of his old teacher. Aristotle had written notes in the margins when the young prince was under the philosopher's instruction.

A vase from ancient Greece depicts the great warrior Achilles in battle. Stories of Achilles in the Iliad *inspired young Alexander.*

village of Mieza. He was schooled in subjects ranging from science to politics to poetry.

He especially enjoyed Aristotle's discussion of the *Iliad*, an epic tale by the poet Homer that recounts

Harsh Rules

Alexander and his classmates in the Royal School of Pages suffered the consequences if they failed to take their training seriously. Philip was known to be a harsh headmaster. He whipped one boy for abandoning an exercise and killed another for disobeying orders. Though severe by today's standards, such punishment was seen by the king as justified. During their last year of training, students served as Philip's bodyguards. To be trusted with the king's life was a great honor. The responsibility required refined soldiering skills and absolute loyalty and obedience.

the Trojan War. According to legend, this conflict occurred in 1200 BCE. It took place between the Greeks and residents of a city called Troy, which was located in present-day Turkey. Alexander was particularly impressed by passages about one of his legendary ancestors, the warrior Achilles. Fearless in the face of death and impressive on the battlefield, Homer's hero was a role model for the young prince.

Yet Alexander did much more than read about glory. He also endured rigorous physical training so that he could one day achieve it. Between the ages of 14 and 18, he was a member of the Royal School of Pages. The school was run by Philip and instructed approximately 50 other boys in military arts such as horsemanship, wrestling, and gymnastics. Alexander proved an accomplished athlete. Once his friends inquired if he would consider participating in the ancient Olympic Games. In his typically bold fashion, Alexander replied, "Yes, if I have kings to run against me."[3]

Alexander admired other people's talents and made a point of learning from their successes. But he also realized that he was no ordinary boy. And he was not brought up to believe any differently. Olympias may have hinted to him that he was not the offspring of the merely mortal Philip. He was the child of the Greek god Zeus. Through Philip's side of the family, he was told he was related to Heracles, or Hercules, a son of Zeus who possessed superhuman strength.

But Alexander did not need such stories to prove that he excelled when it came to his mind, body, and intense ambition. In response, Philip began granting his son increased

Son of the Gods

Religion played a significant role in Alexander's culture. Greeks looked to gods such as Zeus, Hades, Poseidon, and Aphrodite for guidance and protection. People regularly visited sanctuaries that featured temples, altars, and statues constructed for worship. When the Greeks wanted to honor a god or ask for a divine favor, they frequently sacrificed animals such as oxen, goats, and sheep.

Alexander's mother was intensely religious. She acted as a priestess to Dionysus, the god of wine, drama, and fertility. Olympias was apparently so devoted to her duties that she was willing to handle live snakes during certain ceremonies. Some historians argue that she also may have relied upon religion to spur on Alexander's ambition and sense of authority. Plutarch notes how she "confided to him and to him alone" that he was the child of Zeus, the ruler of all the gods.[4] According to this account, Olympias then encouraged Alexander to "show himself worthy of his divine parentage."[5]

political and military responsibilities by the time
Alexander was only 16. The king was taking the final
steps to prepare Alexander for the crown—though
neither man could have known how quickly or
violently it would pass between them. ⌒

An ancient bust of Alexander the Great

Alexander's father, Philip II of Macedonia, on an ancient silver coin

The Final Years of a Father and Son

hilip wasted no time in putting Alexander's obvious talents to good use. The king often entrusted the boy with duties at home while he was away on military campaigns. The prince impressed visiting dignitaries, even those who came from the somewhat mistrusted Persian empire. He was eloquent, intelligent, and appeared comfortable in a leadership position. For these reasons, Philip named Alexander regent in 340 BCE. The king thereby granted his 16-year-old son the power to rule in his absence.

Alexander soon had the opportunity to show that he was just as valuable at Philip's side in battle as he was guarding the throne at home. Philip was pushing for greater control of Greek territories outside Macedonia. In doing so, he angered several city-states, including the powerful and prominent Athens.

In the year that he declared Alexander regent, the king burned a fleet of grain ships bound for Athenian shores. Finally pushed too far, Athens rallied other city-states such as Thebes. They prepared to put a stop to Philip's raging

Early Conquest

As regent, Alexander had far more dangerous and exhausting responsibilities than merely greeting foreign ambassadors. In 340 BCE, a revolt led by a tribe called the Maedi erupted in Macedonia. The rebels were from an ancient country called Thrace, which had become a Macedonian province the year before.

Alexander did not only lead troops to crush the trouble in his kingdom. He also decided to teach the offending tribe a lesson they would never forget. He and his soldiers stormed the Maedi's homeland. According to Plutarch, the young regent then "captured their [principal] city, drove out its barbarous inhabitants, established a colony of Greeks assembled from various regions, and named it Alexandroupolis."[1] Alexandroupolis was the first of many cities founded by Alexander.

Macedonian soldiers in formation carry shields and javelins.

ambition. By 338 BCE, the city-states amassed their forces on a plain in the city of Chaeronea in central Greece.

The Greeks had 35,000 foot soldiers, or hoplites. They outnumbered Philip's forces, which consisted of 24,000 soldiers, by thousands. The city-states were spirited and courageous, but the Macedonian soldiers had extensive training. They also bore the long, deadly, sharp-tipped spear known as the *sarissa*, a weapon introduced by Philip himself.

Philip's army had another advantage, too. This one was less proven in warfare but perhaps just as formidable. Alexander, now 18, played a decisive role in helping his father with the battle. Philip had entrusted his son with the Macedonian cavalry. At a critical moment, Alexander charged through enemy lines. His bold maneuver crushed the Thebans' elite forces, inspiring Philip's men and ultimately leading to victory.

Philip had finally won complete rule over the Greeks, along with all their land and related wealth. In approximately 337 BCE, Philip united the defeated city-states into the Hellenic League. Also called the League of Corinth, the organization allowed members some measure of self-government. Ultimately, however, the league was under Philip's rule and was bound to obey him. It soon became obvious that one such order would be to assist the mighty king in his conquest of the Persian empire.

A Seasoned Warrior

Chaeronea may have marked Alexander's first major military skirmish, but it was one of many in a long line of brutal conflicts for Philip. A ferocious warrior, the king was not without his share of battle scars. In approximately 354 BCE, an arrow pierced Philip's right eye, leaving him with a wound that left him partially blind. He also suffered injuries to his right collar bone, right upper leg bone, and one arm.

A Planned Invasion and a Test of Loyalties

Philip and Alexander shared an unquenchable desire to continue expanding their kingdom. An invasion of Asia would satisfy more than mere ambition. It was also an ideal way to exact revenge on Persia for its attack on Greece more than 150 years earlier. Also, Greek control of eastern lands would result in a bounty of spices, silks, and other exotic treasures. With this in mind, Philip took action in 336 BCE. He ordered his army to advance

Formidable Fighters

Philip's army at Chaeronea did not have the benefit of guns, tanks, or other modern technology, but his troops proved impressive. His infantry fought in a military formation known as a phalanx. This consisted of soldiers grouped close beside each other in rows that ran eight to ten men deep. Some of these fighters, known as *pezhetairoi*, wielded the deadly 13- to 21-foot (4.0- to 6.4-m) *sarissas*. Other infantrymen, called *hypaspistai*, carried shields. Some were trained to throw javelins, spears that were lighter and more slender than the *sarissas*.

Cavalrymen, or *hetairoi*, carried these weapons, as well as lances, or wooden spears with a blade at either end. *Hetairoi* often attacked in a wedge-shaped formation. A commander such as Alexander rode in front to lead the charge into enemy lines. The cavalry was often crucial to victory and was considered the most elite arm of the Macedonian forces. Members of the cavalry underwent extensive instruction so that they had complete control of their steeds and weapons.

Whether on foot or horseback, Macedonian troops formed an incredibly fit, highly efficient killing machine. Few other armies—including the Greek forces at Chaeronea—could boast the professional military schooling that Philip's men brought into battle. Even fewer survived to boast about beating them.

into Asia Minor, which comprised portions of modern-day Turkey.

Unfortunately, Philip and Alexander's shared political ambitions were not enough to shelter them from intense family conflicts. Philip's royal wedding served as the setting for a nearly violent drunken brawl between the two. Philip was already married to several women, including Olympias. However, his union with a beautiful, young Macedonian bride named Cleopatra apparently set Alexander and his mother on edge.

Until that point, there had been little doubt that the 19-year-old prince was next in line to the throne. Nevertheless, several nobles plotted to lay their hands on Philip's growing empire. Cleopatra's uncle, Attalus, was among those attempting to work his family's way into the king's good graces. He offered a wine-sodden, insulting toast at his niece's wedding. Addressing the guests—and possibly Alexander in particular—Attalus asked the crowd to "pray to the gods that the union of Philip and Cleopatra might bring forth a legitimate heir to the throne."[2]

The slight was too much for Alexander, as it cast doubts on his own rights to kingship. The prince attacked Attalus, flinging a goblet at the man's head. In response, Philip stepped in and prepared to draw his sword against his son. However, the king was quite drunk. He stumbled and fell before he could do any physical harm. Upon watching his father crash to the ground, Alexander noted with scorn, "Here is the man who was making ready to cross from Europe to Asia, and [he] cannot even cross from one table to another without losing his balance."[3] The prince saw that his father was deeply enraged and emotionally wounded. He decided it was best to leave Pella temporarily, taking Olympias with him as he departed.

Another Marriage and a Brutal Murder

Before long Philip realized that such a public rift with Alexander was not fitting for a ruling family. They needed to present a unified front to their expansive empire. He invited his son to return home and forged ahead with plans to attack Persian lands. Philip also arranged for the wedding of Alexander's sister. The family would celebrate the occasion with sumptuous feasting and elaborate ceremonies in the Macedonian city of Aegae in the summer of 336 BCE.

The joyous festivities offered no hint of the chaos that was about to occur. That morning, Philip headed into the theater to watch the celebratory athletic games with Alexander close by. Suddenly, an assassin sped to Philip's side and plunged a dagger into the king's ribs. Philip was dead within minutes, and his murderer was killed before he could escape.

Accusations were made regarding motivations for the stabbing. Some said that the attacker was a disgruntled guard who had a dispute with Attalus. The guard was furious with Philip for not punishing Attalus on his behalf. Others, including Alexander, suggested that the Persian king, Darius III, was behind the murder. Some whispered that the prince had conspired with Olympias to bring about Philip's downfall.

Although the pair may not have been responsible, they did take precautions to ensure Alexander's rise to power. Most Macedonian nobles supported Alexander.

A Real Threat to the Throne?

Alexander had demonstrated much promise on the battlefield and in the role of regent. Was it likely that Philip really intended to pass the crown to Cleopatra's son? Most historians consider the notion doubtful. However, others suspect that Olympias's heritage could have worked against the elder prince. While Alexander's mother was of noble birth, she was from the northern kingdom of Epirus. Cleopatra's roots, on the other hand, lay solely in Macedonia. It is possible that some of Philip's countrymen would have preferred to see a pure-blooded Macedonian on the throne, despite their regent's exceptional abilities.

However, a handful of relatives and royals posed
potential competition to Philip's legacy. That group
included Attalus, Cleopatra, and her children, as
Attalus was supporting Cleopatra's son as heir to
the throne. Perhaps not surprisingly, the group was
murdered shortly into Alexander's reign. Alexander
ordered the death of Attalus, while Olympias
handled Cleopatra and her infant son. Such deeds
left a new king with blood on his hands, but the
leadership of an empire was at stake. Alexander
could not afford for his authority to be challenged.
The stakes were too high. He stood to carry out
Philip's planned invasion of Asia and act on his own
incredible ambitions.

An assassin stabs King Philip in the ribs.

Alexander leads the charge into Granicus,
where he won his first major battle in his conquest of Persia.

EARLY ACHIEVEMENTS
ON ASIAN SOIL

ollowing Philip's death, the dream of
conquering the Persian empire may
have continued to consume Alexander's thoughts.
However, the rest of Greece quickly became a
disturbing distraction. Many of the city-states Philip

had united in the League of Corinth had yielded to his will—as opposed to eagerly embracing it. They now celebrated their oppressor's death. Many also decided it was an ideal time to reclaim their independence.

The people of Illyria and Thrace revolted. Alexander stamped out the rebellions in 335 BCE, but similar troubles were far from over. He soon faced unrest in Thebes and lost 500 troops in battle there. In retaliation, his forces demolished the city, killing more than 6,000 of its residents and selling approximately 30,000 people into slavery. The act sent a stern warning to other territories inclined to follow Thebes's example. If Alexander was going to invade Persia successfully, he required absolute obedience from his own countrymen. His actions at Thebes demonstrated that he would tolerate nothing less.

Yet Alexander needed more than fear and submission. He was steps away from leading the largest army a Macedonian ruler had ever commanded into the East. This was largely due to Philip's accomplishments and conquests. It was critical for Alexander to maintain the power of his father's legacy. He needed to gain the support of Macedonia's best officers and most influential nobles. Such men included Antipater, a shrewd, elderly politician. Parmenio and Cleitus were courageous, quick-minded commanders who could aid Alexander as well.

Particularly notable among Alexander's acquaintances was Hephaestion. He had been a classmate of Alexander's, and the pair eventually became close friends. It surprised few that Hephaestion was expected to play a major role in the campaign. As he and many of Alexander's comrades would soon realize, that venture would put their leader's talents to the test—and further reveal his brilliance.

GLORY AT THE GRANICUS

Anxious to finally head eastward, Alexander left for the Persian empire in 334 BCE with more than 37,000 troops. Thousands of additional soldiers were already stationed in Asia Minor.

As Alexander's soldiers advanced, Persian forces prepared for the attack. At least one officer, however, was reluctant to engage Alexander in combat. Memnon was a Greek mercenary who was paid by Darius to command other Greek soldiers fighting for the Persian army. He recommended a "scorched earth" policy, which required that the Persians destroy their own crops and countryside. He argued that this would cut off the enemy's supply of food and other desperately needed provisions. Unsurprisingly, several of the local Persian governors, or satraps, were hesitant to sacrifice their lands. As the Persians would later learn, Memnon's plan would have proven to be wiser than combat. The battle at the Granicus River, in what is now northwestern Turkey, ended in a clear defeat for the Persians.

On the Granicus's eastern shores, more than 40,000 Persian troops readied to destroy Alexander's army. Although outnumbered, the Persians had the advantage of a defensible position. The Macedonians, on the other hand, would have to advance over open ground. The Persians

Greek Mercenaries

Like Memnon, approximately 6,000 of the troops fighting with the Persians at the Granicus were Greek mercenaries, or soldiers paid to serve a country other than their own. The use of such warriors in ancient combat was common. In this particular battle, it was not surprising given that a large number of Greeks resented being ruled by a Macedonian king.

It is possible that many of the Greek mercenaries begged Alexander for mercy when they realized he had the upper hand at the Granicus. If this was indeed the case, their pleas apparently fell on deaf ears. Alexander's forces slaughtered approximately 3,500 Greek mercenaries that day. The massacre made a powerful statement about the loyalty Alexander demanded from his countrymen, as well as the dire penalties they would face if they failed his expectations.

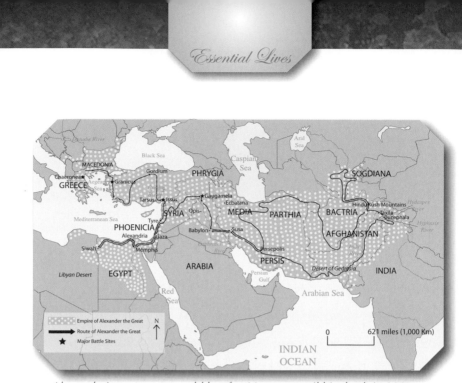

Alexander's conquests would last for 11 years, until his death in 323 BCE. He eventually acquired an empire of unparalleled size.

therefore planned to lead a powerful charge down
the riverbanks while their enemy crossed the deep
and swift water. Meanwhile, Parmenio, realizing
the Persian advantage, counseled Alexander on a
plan of attack. The general advised his young king to
push through the Granicus at dawn. Dawn offered
several advantages: the weak sunlight, the fact that
the enemies would just be awaking, and the Persians'
lack of preparation. But Alexander would not wait
a whole night just to sneak onto soil he intended to
conquer gloriously. He rejected Parmenio's advice.
Instead, he ordered a portion of his troops to enter

the river in broad daylight. This would lure the Persians from their advantageous position on land.

Before long, combat erupted. As javelins fell like rain, the soldiers engaged in bloody, hand-to-hand fighting. Alexander rode Bucephalas into this onslaught. He sported gleaming armor and a helmet with a white feather that made him easily identifiable to his men. Although he sometimes brushed close to death, the 21-year-old emerged victorious. While enemy casualties ranked in the tens of thousands, Alexander lost few more than 115 of his 50,000 men.

At the Granicus, Alexander won the first major conflict in his campaign. The conqueror sent news of his triumph back to Greece in the form of countless slaves and 300 suits of enemy armor. The armor was accompanied by the inscription, "Alexander, son of Philip, together with all the Greeks . . . [presents]

A Complicated Friendship

Alexander had respected Cleitus's military abilities before the Battle of the Granicus, but he had even more reason to appreciate his courage during the course of that conflict. Most historical accounts support the claim that Cleitus saved his commander's life while Alexander battled a Persian officer named Spithridates. According to Arrian, "Spithridates rode up . . . and rising in his stirrups brought down a barbarian battleaxe with all his strength upon Alexander's head. The stroke split the crest of his helmet. . . . But just as Spithridates raised his arm for another blow . . . Cleitus . . . struck first and ran him through with a spear."[1] Ironically, Alexander was ultimately responsible for murdering the man who had protected him when the pair engaged in a drunken, deadly quarrel in 328 BCE.

these tributes, taken from the foreign peoples of
Asia."[2] Such trophies, however, offered only the
faintest glimpse of the victories that would follow.

Overtaking Asia Minor

In the following year, Alexander swept through
Asia Minor. As he progressed, he assumed control
of several cities. Sometimes the satraps and Persian
commanders gave up power peacefully. In other
instances, Alexander was driven to use catapults,
battering rams, and other siege engines to penetrate
city walls. While he was infamously savage, he could
also be practical and political minded. He generally
took pity on those who appeared willing to accept
his rule but who had been forced into battle by their
leaders.

Alexander also allowed the governments he
conquered some measure of independence. In many
cases, however, he stationed his own officials to
ensure that foreign territories remained obediently
aware of his authority. Alexander recognized that
conquered peoples needed to be kept under close
watch. He also recognized they were much less likely
to rebel when allowed to maintain their leaders and
way of life.

More and more, Alexander's dream of capturing the Persian empire appeared to be within his reach. Many believed it was his destiny. In the spring of 333 BCE, Alexander reached Gordium, the capital of Phrygia. Here, he performed a symbolic gesture that would strengthen this belief. He undertook the challenge of untangling the legendary Gordian knot. This complex knot was made from strands of tree bark that had become hardened over time. The wooden knot had

Driven by Divine Will

Alexander was determined to show that he was destined to rule Asia. Prior to departing for the Persian empire, he visited the ancient Greek city of Delphi. The Greeks regarded the location as a sacred shrine to the god Apollo. The god was said to communicate with his oracle, or priestess, there. Alexander supposedly wanted to consult the famed oracle about whether his campaign would be successful. Or perhaps he just wanted an endorsement of his plans. According to legend, he arrived at the shrine in winter, when it was closed. But Alexander was not one to let such details derail him. The great ruler ordered the oracle to appear anyway. When she refused, he himself tried to drag her to the temple. At this, she exclaimed, "You are invincible, my son!"[3] To Alexander's ears, those words comprised the prophecy he had been seeking.

The young king breathed life into such prophecies when he first arrived in Asia. Before he touched ground, he stood on the deck of his ship and cast a spear onto the shore. He then claimed Asia "thenceforward as his own, received from the gods and won by right of conquest."[4] In Alexander's mind, victory was assured because he had divine support. By throwing his spear, he exhibited faith that his control of the Persian empire was truly the gods' will.

supposedly joined a wagon to its yoke for hundreds of years. The knot had frustrated and foiled everyone who had tried to unravel it. Those who had made an attempt were motivated by the prophecy of an oracle. The oracle said that whoever succeeded in undoing the knot would rule Asia.

What He Looked Like

Biographer Peter Green offers the following physical description of the Macedonian king: "Alexander had grown into a boy of rather below average height, but [he was] very muscular. . . . His hair, blond and tousled, is traditionally said to have resembled a lion's mane, and he had that high complexion, which fair-skinned people so often display. His eyes were odd, one being grey-blue and the other dark brown."[6] Many historians tend to agree that the young king was generally attractive. He had an inner intensity that often revealed itself through his expressions, voice, and overall physical appearance.

Most ancient historians believed Alexander simply slashed through the wood with his sword. In any case, Arrian asserts, "When he [Alexander] and his entourage left . . . the wagon, it was as if the oracle [prophecy] of the loosening of the knot had been fulfilled."[5] Whether through fate, skill, or force, Alexander was determined to wield his authority over the world. Darius, however, had other plans for his enemy, and the two men would soon face each other in battle.

Alexander slashes through the fabled Gordian knot with his sword.

*The great Persian leader and Alexander's enemy, Darius,
fled by chariot after his resounding defeat at Issus.*

A CLASH OF KINGS

s Alexander pushed through Asia Minor, he overtook nearly every major city and region in his path. Darius began to grow increasingly disturbed. The Persian king had not been present at the Granicus in 334 BCE. But his rival's swift progress since that conflict was proof that Darius had reason to be concerned. Darius began to assemble massive troops to destroy his enemy.

By late 333 BCE, Darius had gathered an army that may have included as many as 100,000 men. The army was stationed in Babylon, a major Persian city located in what is now Iraq. Realizing that Darius was marching west, Alexander began heading east through Asia Minor to meet the Persians. A difficult and bloody battle lay ahead for the Macedonians, as they were outnumbered by more than two to one. Finally, in the village of Issus, Alexander faced his enemy.

In a surprise move, some of Darius's troops closed in on Alexander from behind. This forced the Macedonian army to react quickly and ferociously. Though they had been taken off guard, the invaders possessed one tactical advantage. The Persians had positioned themselves so that fighting would occur between the Mediterranean Sea and the Amanus Mountains. The narrow

A Dangerous Bath

Ironically, battle wounds were not the only threats to Alexander's well-being. The young commander arrived in the Cilician city of Tarsus in the fall of 333 BCE. He was hot, tired, and eager to refresh himself in the ice-cold Cyndus River. However, this bath nearly resulted in disaster. The freezing water, which trickled from the wintry peaks of the Taurus Mountains, left Alexander chilled. He was racked with fever for several days afterward. Most of his physicians doubted the king would survive, but he proved them wrong. He was fully recovered by the time he confronted Darius at Issus that fall.

battlefield stretched only approximately 1.75 miles (2.82 km) across. This meant that an army as vast as Darius's would be short on space and challenged in its movements.

The night before Alexander's planned attack, he rallied his men. His soldiers were undoubtedly aware that they were badly outnumbered. Recalling their success at the Granicus, he bolstered their courage with the promise of another victory:

> *Remember that already danger has often threatened you, and you have looked it triumphantly in the face; this time the struggle will be between a victorious army and an enemy already once vanquished.*[1]

A Speech Designed to Inspire

While preparing for the battle at Issus, Alexander understood that enemy forces outnumbered his men. It was critical for Alexander to rally his soldiers' spirits and instill them with confidence and the ambition that drove him. To achieve these goals, he reminded his army that many of their opponents were either slaves or mercenaries. These Persian soldiers did not share the freedom or glory that defined his campaign in Asia. According to Arrian, Alexander spoke these words:

> *Our enemies are . . . men who for centuries have lived soft and luxurious lives; we of Macedon . . . have been trained in the hard school of danger and war. Above all, we are free men, and they are slaves. There are Greek troops, to be sure, in Persian service—but how different is their cause from ours! They will be fighting for pay—and not much of it . . . we . . . shall fight for Greece, and our hearts will be in it. And what, finally, of the two men in supreme command? You have Alexander, they—Darius!*[2]

Whether they were motivated by their leader's words or had the tactical advantage, the Macedonians prevailed. Up against terrifying odds, they managed to strike a shattering blow to their foes at Issus. This was due in part to the weakness of the Persian infantry and the strength of the Macedonian cavalry, led by Alexander himself. Although Alexander suffered a leg wound and lost approximately 7,000 troops, Darius fared far worse. He sacrificed thousands more soldiers than did his opponent. Then, close to being captured, the Persian ruler fled the scene. At just 23 years old, Alexander had sent a once-powerful ruler scrambling to recover his empire.

The Aftermath of Issus

When Darius took flight in the fall of 333 BCE, he abandoned far more than a battlefield. His departure provided Alexander with access to seemingly limitless riches. In Darius's base camp the Macedonians found much treasure: weapons, jewelry, silver, and vast amounts of gold. The young commander now had the wealth he needed to maintain his troops and continue his conquest of Asia.

*In a great show of mercy, Alexander spares
the lives of Darius's wife and children.*

Darius also abandoned his family, leaving them to
Alexander's mercy. But Alexander was not inclined
to exact revenge on these innocent relatives, even
though he was still intent upon capturing Darius.
Alexander assured the royal family that they could
keep their titles and would be shown the respect they
deserved. This treatment may not have been due
solely to humane motives. If Alexander were to later
marry into the Persian royal family, his position as
leader of Asia would be legitimized.

Unsurprisingly, he was not moved to take such pity on Darius. Shortly after the Battle of Issus, the fallen king wrote to Alexander. Darius said that if Alexander returned his family, he would pay a large ransom. Darius also offered his friendship to Alexander. He further proposed to allow the Macedonian king to keep many of the conquered Asian territories in exchange for an alliance with Persia. Alexander responded by reminding Darius that he, Alexander, was now the king of Asia. He was to be treated as nothing less. He also warned the somewhat humbled Persian that, despite his best efforts, there was no hiding spot that would keep him safe for long.

Alexander eagerly continued to pursue his enemy. He also realized that his successes at the Granicus and Issus did not make his control of the Persian empire complete. Moving south along the eastern shores of the Mediterranean Sea, he crossed through the ancient countries of Syria and neighboring Phoenicia.

"What It Is to Be a King"

When Alexander entered Darius's abandoned tent following the Battle of Issus, he was astounded by the richness and luxury of his surroundings. According to Plutarch, "He saw that the basins, the pitchers, the baths themselves, and the caskets containing unguents [ointments] were all made of gold and elaborately carved, and [he] noticed that the whole room was marvelously fragrant with spices and perfumes. . . . He [then] turned to his companions and remarked, 'So, this, it seems, is what it is to be a king.'"[3]

By the autumn of 332 BCE, Alexander had besieged several strategically located cities. These included Tyre, in modern-day Lebanon, and Gaza, in what is now Palestinian territory.

Experience had taught him that it was often necessary to deal with conquered peoples harshly if they resisted his influence. Consequently, Alexander resorted to sieges that occasionally lasted several months, such as those at Tyre and Gaza. He also punished those who dared challenge him with the torturous practice of crucifixion. Nonetheless, not everyone regarded the Macedonian ruler as brutal and hostile, as Alexander learned when he arrived in Egypt in late 332 BCE.

ACCOMPLISHMENTS IN EGYPT

The people of the Egyptian city of Memphis welcomed their new conqueror with relatively open arms. They considered him almost as their liberator, because most Egyptians resented the Persians. The Persians had ruled Egypt oppressively for the better part of two centuries. Though Alexander may have looked with disdain upon some Asian territories, he likely held more respect for the culturally rich Memphis. While there, Alexander hosted athletic and artistic competitions. He even showed reverence for native Egyptian gods, a move that helped him win the goodwill of a people whose religion had been mocked by their previous rulers.

In early 331 BCE, Alexander made a pilgrimage to Siwah. This desert oasis was the site of a famous oracle to Zeus-Ammon. Alexander kept secret what he learned from the oracle. However, the priest apparently pleased Alexander, possibly telling him what his mother may have hinted at—that he was the son of Zeus. Just as importantly, the oracle probably implied to the young king that he would one day reign over the entire world.

Regardless of the oracle's exact words, Alexander was quickly fulfilling the promises of greatness. His list of remarkable accomplishments continued to grow. This included the founding

The Journey to Siwah

Alexander's journey to Siwah was not an easy one, but it was one he regarded as blessed by the gods. At one point, he and his men found themselves without water as they faced the scorching desert. Fortunately, just as "their throats were dry and burned," storms showered the group with much-needed rain.[4]

The travelers later became lost. Some ancient biographers allege that two snakes led them safely to the oasis. Others contend that a pair of crows served as guides. Either way, it was easy for Alexander to interpret what may have been natural coincidences as proof that the gods were helping him. The divinities intended for him to reach his destination and hear the oracle speak.

of the city of Alexandria, along the Mediterranean Sea in northern Egypt, in the spring of 331 BCE. Ancient Alexandria became a major port city and was considered a vital center of culture and trade. Even today, Alexandria is Egypt's second-largest city and most expansive seaport. Alexander had already founded several cities that bore his name, including an Alexandria to commemorate his victory at Issus. And Alexander would go on to establish other Alexandrias. But none equaled the Egyptian city. This Alexandria was the first to be so magnificent in stature and so critical to an already historically significant region.

Before leaving Egypt, Alexander journeyed back to Memphis. There, he met with additional troops that would aid him in his campaign against Darius. His experiences in Egypt had instilled him with an added appreciation for all Asia had to offer. It also provided an even greater notion of his incredible—and potentially godlike—invincibility. Still, victory was far from complete. The Persian king remained on the loose, and much of the continent was left to conquer.

Alexander's army passes by the Sphinx and the great pyramids of Egypt.

Alexander's soldiers were the supreme fighters of their day.

INTENT ON
ABSOLUTE GLORY

Alexander headed back to Phoenicia in 331 BCE. He had been in Asia and North Africa for approximately three years. By this point, he had mastered control over much of the Persian empire. But Darius still lived, and he appeared to be mustering forces in order to reclaim his kingdom. It was not long before Alexander received another message from his enemy. This letter contained a tempting offer.

Darius's wife had become pregnant, most likely by Alexander, and had recently died either in childbirth or as the result of a miscarriage. Darius heard the news and, in an emotional state, made a surprisingly generous offer to his enemy. He would grant Alexander 30,000 talents of silver as a ransom for his remaining family members. He gave up claim to all territories west of the Euphrates River. In doing so, the Persian king was essentially cutting his empire in half. Darius would allow Alexander to keep his son as hostage. And finally, Darius proposed that the young king wed one of his daughters. This strategic marriage would enable Alexander to lay claim to the Persian empire without fighting his way through it. All Alexander had to do was to discontinue his hostility toward Darius.

In the end, Alexander refused to sway to his opponent's appeals. After all, Alexander already had plenty of money. Darius's son was already his hostage, and the Macedonian king could marry the Persian princess whenever he pleased.

Some of Alexander's companions questioned the decision. Parmenio went so far as to remark, "If I were Alexander, I should accept what was offered and make a treaty."[1] Alexander, however, had chosen not to settle for the same standards that so easily persuaded other men. He was not content to accept anything less than complete control of Asia. He indicated as much by bluntly responding, "So should I, if I were Parmenio."[2]

Alexander replied to Darius with an ultimatum: Darius could battle the Macedonian's superior forces in a futile attempt to regain power. Or, he could submit to their will and benefit from his rival's mercy. If Darius submitted to Alexander, he would be allowed to keep his throne and high status among the Persians. If he chose battle, he would be shown no mercy.

Alexander soon knew the Persian king's answer: Darius was once again gathering his troops in Babylon.

FATEFUL FIGHTING AT GAUGAMELA

Darius was intent upon giving his enemy a reason to regret his ambition. The Persian king called on soldiers from the northern and eastern regions

*Alexander prays for victory before a key battle
with the Persians at Gaugamela.*

of the empire, which Alexander had yet to fully
overtake. The support he rallied was significant.
One ancient historian estimated that Darius amassed
nearly 1,040,000 men. The actual number was
probably no more than 100,000. In any case, the
Macedonians were clearly outnumbered. Even more
unnerving for Alexander was the fact that Darius
had prepared far more cavalry than usual, perhaps as
many as 40,000.

Darius also prepared to confront Alexander
with a handful of new and deadly military tactics.
This time, his troops had longer swords and

spears to stand up against the Macedonians' *sarissas.*
Approximately 200 of his chariots sported wheels
with scythes. These sharp, curved blades were
certain to rip
apart the flesh of
any humans or
horses unfortunate
enough to come
too close. Also, 15
war elephants from
India would tower
terrifyingly above
the enemy's cavalry.

Darius was
determined that the
intended battlefield
lend itself to his
advantage as well.
This time, he
wanted to ensure
that his massive
army would have
room to maneuver.
He arranged for the
troops to organize

Success by Sunlight

Alexander was a daring risk taker. Parmenio, however, tended to favor tactics that involved a greater sense of caution. To this end, he advised his king to attack the Persians at Gaugamela in the darkness of night. Parmenio reasoned that charging their opponents after sunset would cause chaos among Darius's troops. He also reasoned it would benefit their men to have darkness at least partially conceal how they were so outnumbered.

Alexander disagreed. Experts point to a few possible reasons for his preferring to approach the battlefield during daylight, one of which is pride. According to Plutarch, he responded to Parmenio by exclaiming, "I will not steal my victory."[3] To achieve complete control of Asia, it was necessary for Alexander to seize Darius when all could see. There could be no question of who truly ruled the Persian empire. All would witness that the victor had won on the merits of his own strength and the gods' will.

It is also likely that Alexander's decision was based in military strategy. Night battles followed no set rules. The upper hand could fall to either side. Confusion was an almost certain result of the limited vision his army would face. This was a factor that easily outweighed any potential advantage Alexander held over Darius by making use of the darkness.

at the Plain of Gaugamela, in what is now Iraq. When they were not practicing military drills, the soldiers smoothed out the earth on the open field. This way, the cavalry would face as few obstacles as possible when they charged their opponents.

As Darius took every possible precaution to guarantee victory, Alexander and his men advanced. Upon arriving near Gaugamela, they once more found themselves severely outnumbered, totaling only approximately 47,000. As usual, however, Alexander was not one to shy away from conflict, even when the odds were against him. He expected each of his soldiers to fight fearlessly and to the best of his abilities. The Macedonians had won before, and they would win again.

In early October of 331 BCE, Alexander led the attack at Gaugamela. The combat was fierce. Darius's vast army and surprising weapons undeniably challenged the spirited Macedonians. But at a single, critical moment, Alexander and some of his cavalry

An Inspiring Sign

If Alexander's troops needed encouragement as the Battle of Gaugamela raged on, they had only to look to the sky. This became evident when the camp seer, or prophet, called attention to an eagle flying directly over Alexander's head. That bird was considered to be especially favored by Zeus. Naturally, Alexander insisted that its presence was a promise of victory. The sighting of the eagle was said to have a great effect on Alexander's soldiers. According to Quintus Curtius Rufus, "The men, who had been terrified moments before, were now fired with tremendous enthusiasm and confidence for the fight."[4]

managed to break through a gap in enemy lines. They charged directly at the Persian king. Once again, Darius turned his chariot and fled. And the departure of their leader once again sent the Persian forces into serious disarray and subsequent defeat.

When the Battle of Gaugamela concluded, approximately 50,000 of Darius's troops lay dead. That tally rang out in stark contrast to the mere 1,000 or so warriors that their opponents had lost.

A Brilliant Move

Darius's troops at Gaugamela significantly outnumbered his opponents. How could Alexander possibly prevent his army from being swallowed up by the countless Persians? In a brilliant move, he ordered his men into a trapezoid formation. He positioned the flanks at a 45-degree angle from his front line. That way, the Persian cavalry would be drawn to the sides, leaving a gap in the center of the Persian lines. This setup also allowed Alexander's soldiers to fend off the Persian advance from each of the plain's four sides.

Alexander had demonstrated that no one could defeat him or dispute his solitary control of the Persian empire. He had achieved a victory that history would never forget.

Exploring an Empire

Following the fighting at Gaugamela, Darius hurried east, accompanied by a fraction of his army. Alexander was fast on his heels. During the course of the pursuit, Alexander stopped in some of the Persian empire's greatest cities. These included Babylon and Susa, located in what is now Iran. While Darius

ran, Alexander and his men basked
in the luxury that the Asian monarch
had been forced to abandon. Many
of the people Alexander encountered
probably realized that it was best to
accept their new conqueror rather
than fight him. Alexander essentially
enjoyed a hero's welcome.

Perhaps even more pleasing,
however, was the wealth that seemed
to fall at his feet. Exotic perfumes
and spices, caged beasts such as
leopards and lions, and thousands
of talents of gold and silver were at his disposal.
Additionally, more soldiers were on their way from
Macedonia. Alexander received nearly 15,000
additional troops by the end of 331 BCE. These
soldiers proved valuable as the young king journeyed
to the ancient Persian province of Persis, in the
southwestern portion of present-day Iran. Persis was
the homeland of Darius and his royal ancestors. It
also encompassed the city of Persepolis, the capital of
the mighty Persian empire—and Alexander's target.

As he headed southeast, he was forced to battle
everyone from aggressive mountain tribesmen called

Image Control

Alexander may have tow-
ered over Darius in battle.
However, he certainly did
not overshadow the Per-
sian king when it came
to height. Upon sitting on
Darius's throne in Susa,
Alexander quickly discov-
ered he was shorter than
his enemy. The mighty
conqueror's legs hung
in midair until a servant
placed a small table un-
derneath his feet.

Uxians to the combative satrap of Persis. Alexander forcibly and violently subdued these resistors. In early 330 BCE, he finally reached Persepolis. He authorized his men to pillage the city, allowing them to steal from and murder its residents. From the perspective of Alexander and his troops, theirs was the ultimate act of revenge for Persia's invasion of Greece 160 years earlier. He and his army spent approximately four months in Persepolis. During this time, they captured the expansive treasury and burned the palaces of the once-powerful Persian kings.

By late spring, Alexander decided to resume his hunt for Darius. He left Persis and journeyed northwest. He had long been aggravated that the fallen ruler "was more successful in flight than he himself was in pursuit."[5] And it was not in Alexander's nature to willingly accept defeat.

Alexander the Great has been a favorite subject of artists throughout the ages. This painting is by an Italian artist, circa 1500.

Alexander discovers the body of his great enemy, Darius, king of Persia.

BITTERSWEET SUCCESSES

When Darius fled Gaugamela, he journeyed southeast to Ecbatana, in what is now Iran. The Persian ruler was willing to face Alexander again if he could gather sufficient troops. Until then, however, Darius had no option but to keep one step ahead of his enemy. He was successful in this endeavor for a time. He departed Ecbatana just three days before Alexander was due to arrive.

In the summer of 330 BCE, however, Darius was kidnapped by a group of his own men. The Persian satrap Bessus and some of his companions did not believe that the twice-defeated Darius was an effective leader any longer. Alexander learned from Persian nobles that the king was being held captive. He drove his soldiers even harder, sometimes forcing them to march all night. At last, Alexander was very close to capturing the man who had challenged his rule and evaded him time and again.

But Alexander was not to have the pleasure of deciding Darius's fate. Bessus and his officials had taken their hostage to Parthia, in the northeastern portion of present-day Iran. As Alexander closed in, the men stabbed Darius. They fled shortly before Macedonian troops caught up to the dying king. Alexander was deeply angered by the turn of events. Even so, the young conqueror sent Darius's body back to Persepolis. Alexander's former adversary would "be buried in the royal tombs, just like the kings who had preceded him."[1] Alexander was not beneath honoring his foe in death, even if he had ferociously sought to overthrow him in life.

Darius was dead, but Alexander's work in Asia was far from done. The conqueror next planned to pursue the dead king's assassins. His stated purpose was to avenge the death of the Persian ruler, who had been treated with great dishonor. Perhaps Alexander also took offense at the undignified manner in which Darius had been so savagely murdered. In truth, though, Alexander primarily resented any threat to his own authority. Darius's killers had performed the ultimate offense by refusing to acknowledge Alexander as king of Asia.

The assassins had escaped farther east, where certain other disobedient Persian allies lived. Disloyal sentiments had no place in the world that the 26-year-old Macedonian had battled so hard to master. And, any suspected lack of obedience carried a high price—as some of his closest companions would soon discover.

Tracking an Assassin and Troubled by Treason

As Alexander progressed eastward, some of Darius's killers surrendered. Bessus, however, remained on the loose and proved to be a threat. In the country of Bactria, located in parts of present-day Afghanistan and neighboring areas, Bessus was rallying soldiers in the hopes of eventually overcoming the Macedonians. In response, Alexander fearlessly sought out this new enemy.

Alexander was still held in high esteem by the vast majority of his troops. However, by the early fall of 330 BCE, he was beginning to spark controversy among them. Perhaps in an effort to better fit his role as king of all Asia, Alexander started wearing Persian attire and practicing traditional Persian customs. He even engaged Persian soldiers—including Darius's own brother—as his bodyguards. Many of his Macedonian and Greek companions failed to share his admiration of foreign culture. They also had trouble accepting their former enemies as fellow soldiers. In addition, a fair percentage of the men were homesick. They possibly questioned their leader's reasons for remaining

A Leader and a Soldier, Too

Alexander could drive his men hard. As his army traveled toward Bactria, the troops often struggled with a harsh climate, supply shortages, and grueling marches. Yet Alexander was not one to set himself above his soldiers' suffering. According to one ancient historian, the king would not satisfy his own thirst if his men had no water. "I cannot bear to drink alone," said Alexander when he was offered a cup, "and it is not possible for me to share so little with everybody."[2]

in Asia now that the original goal of conquering Persia had been achieved.

During this time, trouble arose regarding a Macedonian officer named Philotas, who was Parmenio's son. Philotas was accused of failing to inform the king of a suspected plot against his life. After torturing a confession out of the nobleman, Alexander arranged for his execution. He then proceeded to order Parmenio killed as well. Philotas's intentions for not immediately revealing what he knew are uncertain, and Parmenio's love for his son probably made his own death somewhat of a political necessity. Alexander lost a trusted general and a valued friend. The incident would not be the last of its kind as he struggled to balance enormous power and complicated politics with his personal relationships.

Forging ahead, he continued his hunt for Bessus. In the spring of 329 BCE, Alexander and his men endured the steep, snowy Central

A Friend in Trouble

In 330 BCE, during his pursuit of Bessus, Alexander conducted a successful campaign against the Mardian tribe. But his victory nearly cost him a dear friend. A handful of his foes managed to launch an unexpected attack and capture his beloved horse, Bucephalas. As Plutarch described it, "Alexander was enraged and sent a herald with the threat that, unless they gave back his horse, he would exterminate the whole tribe, together with their women and children."[3] His threat did not fall on deaf ears. The stallion was soon returned along with several gifts and some 50 Mardians pleading for forgiveness.

*Bessus of Bactria hangs on a cross as punishment
for daring to defy the great Alexander.*

Asian mountain system known as the Hindu Kush.
The Macedonians crossed the mountain range in
just 17 days. They pressed on into Bactria, where
Bessus finally fell into their grasp. Just as Bessus
had turned on Darius, so did a handful of Persian
noblemen betray the rebellious satrap to Alexander.
Under the Macedonian king's supervision, Bessus
was tortured and executed, possibly on a cross. But
the brutal death of Bessus failed to entirely eliminate
Alexander's troubles, as the events of the next few
years would show.

A Time of Unrest and Regret

The lands Darius had once controlled were vast. Alexander was rapidly discovering that winning the favor of everyone in his new empire would not be an easy task. By the fall of 329 BCE, one of Alexander's primary challenges was to put down revolts in Bactria and the nearby province of Sogdiana. He also faced unrest in a region known as Scythia, which stretched between the Black and Aral seas.

These areas presented a starkly

A Conflict of Cultures

Alexander demonstrated that he could straddle the cultures of two vastly different worlds—Europe and Asia. Officers such as Parmenio and Cleitus were likely ill pleased when he "put on the Persian diadem [crown] and dressed himself in the white robe [and] the Persian sash."[4] Clothes, however, were one thing, while certain Persian customs were quite another.

Alexander soon began advocating a Persian tradition known as *proskynesis*. This tradition required his subjects to bow deeply or even lie face downward to express their admiration. Such a display was common in Persia, but in Greece it was performed only during godly worship. The commander's divine ancestry may have been hinted at in the past. However, his companions secretly disliked the idea of treating him like a living god.

The ancient historian Callisthenes openly objected to his king's suggested use of *proskynesis*. "For my part," Callisthenes observed, "I hold Alexander fit for any mark of honor that a man may earn, but do not forget that there is a difference between honoring a man and worshipping a god."[5] The historian's straightforward opinion caused him to fall out of royal favor. However, it also prompted Alexander to reconsider his position. In the end, the king imposed *proskynesis* only on Asian peoples.

different environment from the banquet halls of Babylonia and the palaces of Persepolis. Such areas boasted aggressive, unpredictable warriors and rugged land. Alexander's men struggled to meet the challenges of their enemy. They sometimes relied on siege engines such as catapults to achieve victory.

In addition to the difficulties of combat, Alexander was haunted by a mistake he would deeply regret. In the autumn of 328 BCE, he was attending a banquet with some of his officers. As the men drank, tensions deepened between Alexander and Cleitus, one of his commanders.

Cleitus clearly disapproved of several of the leader's decisions. He also failed to understand Alexander's growing attachment to Asia. Cleitus's displeasure ranged in scope from the king's new clothes to the foreigners he selected for military posts. Nor did he grasp how so many of his companions could shamelessly flatter their commander. Their flattery had made the conqueror seemingly forget that their

Fateful Words

More and more, several of Alexander's troops were irritated by what they saw as the king's growing arrogance and unpatriotic adoption of Asian culture. Cleitus pushed his king to recognize the role his countrymen had played in his numerous successes and to recall their shared heritage. "It is by the blood of these Macedonians," he argued, "and by their wounds that you have become so great that you disown your father Philip and make yourself the son of Ammon [Zeus]."[6]

entire army—and not just Alexander—had triumphed over Darius.

At one point, others present suggested that Philip, whom Cleitus had also faithfully served, had failed to match his son in greatness. At that, the hostility erupted into chaos. Cleitus furiously disagreed with the assertion about Philip. He also attempted to humble his ruler by recalling how he, Cleitus, had saved the young king's life at the Battle of the Granicus. Unfortunately, the reminder only stung Alexander's pride and increased his rage. Unwilling to tolerate further insults, the intoxicated king stabbed Cleitus with a pike. Once again, Alexander had killed one of his own valuable officers. The drunken act left him immobilized by guilt for several days.

Cleitus was not alone in his poor view of Alexander. Many others also disapproved of the king's thinly veiled vanity and his ruthless ambition. Alexander often drove those around him at an inhuman pace, accepting nothing less than total obedience. He insisted on being treated like the mighty king of a magnificent empire—and, as some whispered, a god over all humanity.

Alexander murders Cleitus in a drunken rage.

Alexander marries Roxane, a Bactrian noblewoman.

ENDLESS AMBITION
IN INDIA

Alexander grieved over Cleitus, and ongoing revolts in territories such as Bactria and Sogdiana cast darkness on the leader's glory. Nonetheless, he began preparing for new campaigns by 327 BCE. After finally putting down much of the unrest, he appointed a Macedonian satrap to maintain order in the unruly areas.

Alexander also continued to mix European and Asian cultures. He started training perhaps as many as 30,000 local Asians to serve in his army. He also married Roxane, the daughter of a Bactrian nobleman whom the Macedonians had once taken prisoner. Several of Alexander's countrymen were unsettled by the idea of their commander choosing a wife they considered little better than a barbarian. But the 28-year-old monarch seemed genuinely in love. He and Roxane wed in the spring of 327 BCE, but the king had no thoughts of giving up further exploits for the comfort of domestic life.

Alexander and his men set out for the Indus River and prepared for their next intended conquest—India. Darius had considered the Indus Valley a province of the Persian empire. The vast area stretched over lands that now comprise India as well as Pakistan, Afghanistan, and Turkmenistan.

Darius had enjoyed the abundance of gold that came from that region. As the new master of Darius's kingdom, Alexander was eager to explore the area with the goal of taking his troops to the easternmost borders of Asia.

In the spring of 326 BCE, Alexander's men arrived at the Indus River. They prepared for their crossing by constructing a bridge and organizing ships and boats. This passage would be just one adventure among many. Those to follow would be filled with exotic riches and unexpected risks.

Heavy Fighting on the Hydaspes

Alexander arrived on the river's eastern shores to be greeted with great flourish by a native ruler. Taxiles was the king of the city of Taxila, in what is now northern Pakistan. Taxiles peacefully surrendered his territory to the Macedonians and showered the invaders with gifts ranging from elephants to silver. But Taxiles' response to a new ruler was in no way an indication of what lay ahead.

As far as an Indian king named Porus was concerned, the Macedonian commander deserved far less than a hero's welcome. Porus ruled over a wealthy kingdom in what is now Pakistan. However, he refused to hand over the riches Alexander demanded as a tribute. Instead, Porus gathered approximately 22,000 warriors and as many as 200 elephants. Porus's aim was to prevent the Macedonians from crossing the Hydaspes River.

Porus held the advantage of being able to attack the enemy as they waded through the waterway. Alexander, however, had almost twice as many soldiers, as well as his notable talent for military strategy.

Alexander and Porus prepared to battle in May of 326 BCE. Before Alexander crossed the Hydaspes, he led his forces back and forth along the river several times. This constant movement was part of an effort to confuse the Indians about where he actually planned to cross. Alexander also divided his army. He wanted Porus to be faced with a nearly impossible decision about which group of Macedonians to confront once fighting began. When warfare did erupt, the smell, sound, and size of the Indians' elephants terrified the Macedonians' horses. However, the giant creatures probably harmed Porus just as much as they helped him. The beasts, many of which had lost their riders, went out of control. They trampled fighters on both sides of the conflict.

An Unlikely Friendship

Though Alexander may not have known it when he first looked upon Porus, he and the fallen Indian king were destined to become great allies. The two monarchs ultimately found they trusted and respected one another sufficiently to form a long-lasting and productive partnership. Alexander still demanded ongoing tribute from Porus after he departed India. However, the local ruler was permitted to reign over the extensive lands between the Himalayas and the Indian Ocean. Ironically, their previous conflict left both men with greater kingdoms than they had possessed before their battle.

The Indian king Porus surrenders to Alexander.

Alexander and his soldiers endured a challenging battle, made all the worse by the rainstorms that turned the battlefield to mud. But in the end, they surrounded Porus and his men, prompting their surrender.

The victors lost approximately 4,000 of their troops. Also, their commander was forced to bid farewell to Bucephalas. Porus was left to cope with 12,000 casualties, including both his sons. When Alexander came face-to-face with the Indian prince, he asked him, "What do you wish me to do with you?"[1] Dignified even if defeated, Porus answered, "Treat me, O Alexander, like a king."[2] The mighty

Macedonian conqueror was pleased with this show of respect and honor. He allowed Porus to keep his throne, made him an ally, and granted him additional territories to rule.

As this exchange made evident, Alexander was not without mercy if an enemy impressed him and the terms of reconciliation were to his liking. But sometimes he was unaware that not everyone shared his lofty goals. He would soon learn the limits of soldiers who were eager for home and exhausted by his ambition. The battle of the Hydaspes was to be his last major campaign.

ANOTHER INDIAN RIVER AND A NEW FORM OF RESISTANCE

For Alexander, the march east toward the Hyphasis River was by no means simple. But it was filled with intriguing new plants and animals, not to mention additional lands to which he laid claim. His men, however, were weary from the fierce fighting at the Hydaspes. They had had their fill of venomous snakes, drenching monsoons, impassable rivers, and aggressive tribesmen. By now, they had marched well over 15,000 miles (24,000 km). Would their king never be satisfied?

Towering Testimonies

Alexander oversaw the construction of 12 altars to Greek gods at the Hyphasis River. These represented his effort not only to display religious reverence but also to mark the geographic boundaries of his empire. Though the structures have never been located, each one is estimated to have been approximately 75 feet (23 m) tall.

From Alexander's perspective, their work was far from over. During a speech to his forces in the late summer of 326 BCE, he described how they would forge past the Ganges River to the Indian Ocean. Then they would continue onward. He said:

Our ships will [then] sail round from the Persian Gulf to Libya. All Libya to the eastward will soon be ours, and all Asia, too, and to this empire there will be no boundaries but what God Himself has made for the whole world.[3]

Alexander promised them greater glory and treasure than they could possibly imagine if they pressed ahead with him. But the men refused to go any farther. Finally, a senior officer named Coenus spoke for the troops:

I judge it best to set some limit to further enterprise. . . . Do not try to lead men who are unwilling to follow you; if their heart is not in it, you will never find the old spirit or the old courage.[4]

Though Coenus's words were spoken respectfully, they stirred deep anger in Alexander. The king withdrew to his tent for days. For once, he was forced to swallow defeat. His warriors shouted his praises when he finally announced they would return home.

The journey homeward was full of hardship. Alexander was intent to make the most of the trip back. He put his recently reinforced army—totaling approximately 120,000 men—to good use. As his forces swept southwest toward the Indus, intense fighting ensued with several local peoples. They included a tribe known as the Mallians, whom the Macedonians confronted in early 325 BCE.

While battling this group,

An Immovable Audience

Alexander's words to his troops at the Hyphasis River failed to win their enthusiasm for future ventures into Asia. The men were unmoved regardless of whether his tone was encouraging or enraged. Before Coenus expressed his hesitation regarding additional eastward progress, the king tried to raise his soldiers' spirits with an inspiring speech. He urged:

Stand firm, for well you know that hardship and danger are the price of glory and that sweet is the savor of a life of courage and of deathless renown beyond the grave.[5]

But when the men demonstrated that they much preferred Coenus's reasoning, Alexander addressed them in another manner. He warned:

I shall have others who will need no compulsion to follow their king. If you wish to go home, you are at liberty to do so—and you may tell your people that you deserted your king in the midst of his enemies.[6]

Despite his efforts, Alexander would regain his army's loyalty only when he promised they would return to their homeland.

A Show of Leadership

Alexander's wound from a Mallian arrow caused him intense discomfort, but he was forced not to show any weakness. His army was already floundering amid mass panic and confusion at the rumor that he had died. To crush this rumor, he overcame his pain and appeared before his troops atop his steed. According to Arrian, "At the sight of him once more astride his horse, there was a storm of applause so loud that the riverbanks . . . reechoed with the noise. . . . Wreaths were flung upon him and such flowers as were then in bloom."[7] His soldiers may have questioned his ambition at the Hyphasis River. However, they realized that they stood little chance of making it back to Macedonia alive without their fearless commander.

Alexander was wounded by an arrow that pierced his lung. Though he survived, the injury was more significant than any other he had suffered. The Mallians, however, fared far worse. Like anyone foolish enough to resist Alexander, they endured his wrath. They were either slaughtered or enslaved.

As they continued the return trip, the Macedonians still met with occasional hostility. They also encountered several native kings who preferred to accept their leader rather than risk his vengeance. By then, anyone who had heard the name Alexander knew of his countless accomplishments. All were aware that he would take whatever measures were necessary to control the world he had created for himself. ⌐

A mosaic from 200 BCE depicts Alexander in battle.

Chapter 9

A silver coin showing Alexander was used as currency during his reign.

NEVER ANOTHER LIKE HIM

By the summer of 325 BCE, Alexander and his men were preparing to progress farther west and into the final stages of their homeward journey. The king divided his forces into three groups, with each group following a different westward route. Alexander and his portion of troops planned to travel through the ancient region of Gedrosia, in present-day southern Pakistan. The area was known for its treacherous desert climate. Many a traveler had attempted to pass through and had failed. Unsurprisingly, Alexander was determined to succeed where others had merely struggled. He anticipated a challenge, and Gedrosia certainly lived up to his expectations.

Like Alexander, some of his soldiers had married native women during the course of the expedition. And some of these marriages had produced children. Now Alexander's soldiers traveled with the families they had started in Asia. The travelers endured everything from arid heat and frequent lack of water to intense monsoons, fast-moving floods, and fierce sandstorms. Sadly, the difficult march proved fatal for many of the

Crossing "Oceans of Sand"

Alexander and his troops quickly discovered that Gedrosia had not earned its ominous reputation on the basis of mere rumors. They faced scorching heat, lethal monsoons, and shifting sands. As if that were not enough, their guides at one point confessed that they were lost in the stark wilderness. According to Arrian, those who survived each passing day were all but driven mad by the disastrous conditions. Thousands more perished like "poor castaways in the ocean of sand."[1]

warriors' new wives and children as well as thousands of Alexander's own men.

But Alexander accomplished yet another challenge that may have seemed unachievable to others. He crossed Gedrosia in only two months. At about the same time, he became greatly displeased to hear reports regarding some of his appointed satraps and officers at various foreign posts. Complaints had arisen that both Macedonian and Persian men were misusing their authority to rob and occasionally even murder the local citizens under their control.

Alexander was responsible for maintaining order over a vast empire. He could not afford for those he empowered to abuse his trust or cause any unrest. To send a message that such behavior was unacceptable, he ordered the execution of thousands of alleged offenders in 325 BCE. Despite this wave of bloodshed, the year did not end on a completely unhappy note. By early winter, Alexander's army was reunited. Yet while Alexander and his troops inched ever closer to Macedonia, he continued to demonstrate his appreciation for Asian culture. He would soon offer proof of this affection by extending his royal family.

MATRIMONY, MUTINY, AND MOURNING

The Macedonians reached the great Persian city of Susa in February of 324 BCE. Shortly after arriving, Alexander arranged for an elaborate wedding ceremony. The lavish party may have upset more people than it impressed. The mass marriage linked the commander and approximately 90 of his leading friends and officers to women of Persian royalty. It signified that the future rulers of his empire would claim both Asian and European bloodlines. Alexander himself wed two Persian noblewomen, including Darius's eldest daughter, Stateira.

Many of his men, however, were upset by his continuing efforts to mix their civilization with that of the Asians they had conquered. They believed that his generosity to Asians took away from their own status. For example, the king had made a

Alexander's Sons

Though Alexander had three wives after the mass marriage at Susa, he fathered only two confirmed children during his lifetime. Both died before they produced sons of their own, ending Alexander's bloodline. Born in 327 or 326 BCE, Herakles was his son by Barsine, a woman Alexander had never officially wed. Alexander IV, born in 323 BCE, was his son by Roxane. The boy was regarded as heir to his father's kingdom, though other men ruled in his place due to his young age. Both Alexander IV and Herakles were potential threats to rising politicians hoping to seize power. As a result, Alexander IV was killed when he was approximately 13, and Herakles when he was 18. Their murders were driven by motives similar to those that had led to the elimination of Alexander's half brother after Philip's death in 336 BCE.

grand gesture by paying any debts the soldiers had accumulated during his Asia campaign. But he had also taken steps to provide a Macedonian education and military training to tens of thousands of foreigners.

The final straw came that summer, when Alexander arrived in the city of Opis, in what is now Iraq. After he ordered that all older or disabled soldiers were to be sent home and paid for their services, the troops mutinied. They openly challenged Alexander. How could he dismiss them so casually after all they had suffered for his sake?

A Stern Scolding at Opis

Alexander had reluctantly relented during the mutiny at the Hyphasis River. However, he would not bend to the wishes of his soldiers at Opis. His men were not shy about expressing their displeasure at his plans to retire certain troops. In response, Alexander furiously reminded them how humble their lives had been before he and Philip had raised them to the rank of triumphant conquerors. He also insisted that he had endured hardship alongside the best of them. He recalled how he had frequently sacrificed his own comfort and safety to see to their needs, saying:

Does any man among you honestly feel that he has suffered more for me than I have suffered for him? There is no part of my body but my back which has not a scar. . . . I have sword-cuts from close fight; arrows have pierced me, missiles from catapults [have] bruised my flesh; again and again I have been struck by stones or clubs—and all for your sakes: for your glory and your gain. Over every land and sea, across river, mountain, and plain I [have] led you to the world's end, a victorious army.[2]

Alexander became enraged at this show of disrespect. He would not again give in to the men's complaints as he had at the Hyphasis River. This time, he could afford to replace any troublemakers with foreign soldiers. He therefore responded to the revolt by executing its primary ringleaders. Those troops who survived his wrath received a stern reminder of all he and his father had done to add to their personal wealth and glory. If they chose to show their gratitude by abandoning him, they were free to go. His countrymen were shocked and scared at the realization that they were, in fact, dispensable. They pleaded for his forgiveness. In an emotional display that revealed how much Alexander did indeed value the warriors, he tearfully extended his pardon and embraced them as his kin.

These tears would not be his last. By fall, Alexander had made his way to Ecbatana. Here he arranged for athletic and dramatic competitions, as well as elaborate banquets. During the course of the festivities, his fellow officer Hephaestion fell ill with a fever. Alexander's dear friend died just days later. Devastated by this loss, Alexander attempted to distract himself by pushing toward Babylon. His aim was to subdue a tribe known as the Cossaeans in the mountains of present-day Iran. According to Plutarch, he massacred "the whole male population from the youths upwards . . . [as] a sacrifice to the spirit of Hephaestion."[3] Though Alexander could not have known it then, it would be less than a year before he himself would serve as the subject of widespread mourning.

UNREALIZED DREAMS AND A CONQUEROR'S DEATH

Alexander did not return to Macedonia before his death. He managed to get as far west as Babylon by the spring of 323 BCE. He then busied himself preparing an enormous fleet. The ships were for his intended conquest of Arabia, a region in southwest Asia comprised of present-day Saudi Arabia and neighboring countries. It is possible that he also had plans to invade other portions of the Mediterranean. He envisioned building magnificent cities, roads, temples, and pyramids throughout his massive empire. He would continue mingling various world cultures.

Whatever his final ambitions may have been, they were not realized during his lifetime. Alexander became ill in May of 323 BCE and died that June. Theories about his death continue more than 2,000

*Soldiers pay their final respects to Alexander the Great.
He died in Babylon in 323 BCE at the age of 32.*

years later. Some historians believe he was poisoned.
Others suggest his end was connected to a disease
called malaria, the lung wound he received in India,
or years of excessive drinking. Many ancient reports
indicate that he became ill following another bout of
decadent feasting. Another story goes that the illness
was triggered by an especially large goblet of wine.
According to this account, he cried out sharply as
soon as he had downed the last gulp. He then lay on
his sickbed for several days.

The King's Body

Why wasn't Alexander buried in his home country? Some historians believe his remains were initially sent to Macedonia. But the conqueror's body had to be transported through several regions in Asia before it reached that destination. Alexander had left very vague instructions regarding who should rule his kingdom. So many of these areas were rapidly being claimed by nobles and generals competing for a piece of the empire.

Some experts suggest that Ptolemy I Soter, a Macedonian officer who had taken control of Egypt, intercepted Alexander's corpse. He did so in order to assert his own authority. Macedonian customs suggested that burying a dead monarch was a means of establishing oneself as his successor. This might explain why Ptolemy insisted his former commander be laid to rest in Alexandria. Ptolemy did then go on to found a powerful Egyptian dynasty that lasted for more than 300 years.

During his final hours, everyone from ordinary soldiers to court officials paraded past him to pay their respects. Shortly before he died, he was asked who should inherit his vast kingdom. Alexander responded that he willed it "to the strongest man."[4] On June 10, the 32-year-old who was regarded as king and god, conqueror and legend, breathed his last breath. According to tradition, he was buried in Alexandria, Egypt, but archaeologists have yet to locate his remains.

Alexander's generals and nobles were left to decide for themselves who possessed the most strength. In the end, they failed. The hoped-for unity of Alexander's kingdom disappeared upon his death. His successors divided up the extensive territories he had dedicated his entire existence to overtaking. Throughout the next several decades, they founded their own empires and crushed anyone who stood in their path. This included Roxane and a son she gave birth to not long after her husband died. Chaos and political competition inevitably followed the end of Alexander's reign. But certain aspects of his legacy proved indestructible.

While in Asia, Alexander did far more than conquer enemy cities. His presence effectively spread Hellenistic culture, including Greek language, customs, government policies, and military techniques. And, regardless of his countrymen's distaste for Asian influence during his reign, he also immersed Greece in the rich traditions of that continent. Entire global populations, as well as countless historic rulers, can claim a heritage that was given shape by European and Asian bloodlines mixed during Alexander's campaigns.

Perhaps just as powerful, however, was the standard he set for future leaders. He inspired men and women

Big Shoes to Fill

As Julius Caesar made his way through Spain in 69 BCE, he reportedly wept upon seeing a statue of Alexander. Then about 31, the Roman was filled with both amazement and envy at a conqueror who had achieved control over most of the known world at approximately the same age. The story goes that Caesar's tears were a result of his realization of how little he had accomplished in comparison to the famed Macedonian.

as remarkable in their own right as Rome's Julius Caesar and Egypt's Queen Cleopatra. Alexander did not only display incredible ambition. He also possessed the talent and intelligence to transform his goals into realities. Both formidable and marvelous, he was truly nothing if not great. As Arrian spoke of him:

> *It is my belief that there was in those days no nation, no city, no single individual beyond the reach of Alexander's name; never in all the world was there another like him.*[5]

A statue of Alexander the Great in modern Greece pays tribute to the ancient leader.

TIMELINE

356 BCE	ca. 344 BCE	342 BCE to 338 BCE
Alexander III is born to King Philip II and Queen Olympias in the ancient kingdom of Macedonia in July.	Alexander astounds spectators, including his father, by taming the unruly stallion Bucephalas.	Alexander receives military and physical training alongside the sons of other Macedonian nobles at the Royal School of Pages.

335 BCE	334 BCE	333 BCE
Alexander forcefully puts down revolts in Illyria and Thebes.	Alexander's first major victory against the Persians occurs at the Battle of the Granicus River in the spring.	In the spring, Alexander unties the fabled Gordian knot and thus reaffirms his destiny to become ruler of all Asia.

338 BCE

Alexander fights beside his father in a stunning victory over the Greek city-states during the Battle of Chaeronea in August.

337 BCE

Philip and Alexander quarrel at a banquet following the king's wedding to Cleopatra, prompting the prince to leave home temporarily.

336 BCE

In summer, Philip is assassinated in Aegae, and Alexander takes the throne.

333 BCE

Alexander confronts and defeats Darius's troops at the Battle of Issus in November; Darius subsequently flees.

331 BCE

In April, Alexander founds the city of Alexandria, Egypt.

331 BCE

Macedonians triumph over Persians at Gaugamela in October; Darius flees once more.

TIMELINE

330 BCE

Persian conspirators, including a satrap named Bessus, murder Darius in July.

330 BCE

In the fall, Philotas and his father, Parmenio, are executed.

329 BCE

In the spring, Alexander and his men cross the Hindu Kush in 17 days.

326 BCE

In May, Alexander wages a successful attack on an Indian king named Porus at the Battle of the Hydaspes.

326 BCE

In late summer, Alexander's exhausted army mutinies at the Hyphasis River; he reluctantly agrees to begin the journey homeward.

325 BCE

In the winter, Alexander is wounded by an arrow to his lung as he battles an Indian tribe known as the Mallians.

329 BCE

Alexander captures Bessus in the summer and authorizes his torture and execution.

328 BCE

Alexander murders Cleitus with a pike after a drunken quarrel; he is subsequently crippled with guilt.

327 BCE

Alexander marries a Bactrian princess named Roxane and begins planning his invasion of India.

324 BCE

In a mass marriage ceremony in February, Alexander links himself and 90 of his leading friends and officers to Persian nobles.

324 BCE

In the summer, Alexander's troops mutiny at Opis; Alexander harshly quashes his opponents.

323 BCE

On June 10, Alexander dies in Babylon at the age of 32.

Essential Facts

Date of Birth

July, 356 BCE

Place of Birth

Macedonia, an ancient kingdom north of Greece

Date of Death

June 10, 323 BCE

Marriages

Alexander was married to three women at one time. He married the Bactrian princess Roxane out of love in 327 BCE. Then, three years later, he married two additional Persian wives in order to secure important political connections.

Children

Alexander fathered two confirmed sons, Herakles, born 327 or 326 BCE, and Alexander IV, born in 323 BCE. Both sons were killed as teenagers by politically motivated rivals.

Conquests

Alexander's life ambition was to conquer the Persian empire, and he took over vast portions of the region before his death. His empire stretched from Macedonia and Greece in the west all the way to the Indian subcontinent in the east, including parts of North Africa and the Middle East. See map page 38.

KEY BATTLES

❖ Battle of Chaeronea; Philip and Alexander conquer the Greek city-states, 338 BCE.

❖ Battle of the Granicus; Alexander's first major victory against the Persians, 334 BCE.

❖ Battle of Issus; Alexander defeats his rival, King Darius of Persia, 333 BCE.

❖ Battle of Gaugamela; another victory over Darius, 331 BCE.

❖ Battle of the Hydaspes; Alexander defeats Indian king Porus, 326 BCE.

PERSONALITY

Alexander had a ferocious appetite for world domination and a remarkable talent for military strategy. He also showed a fascination for foreign cultures that sometimes riled his Greek companions. Alexander was known to be both ruthless and, at times, overwhelmingly compassionate. On at least one occasion, his fierce temper led him to murder a dear friend—an act he would bitterly regret.

QUOTE

"Does any man among you honestly feel that he has suffered more for me than I have suffered for him? There is no part of my body but my back which has not a scar. . . . I have sword-cuts from close fight; arrows have pierced me, missiles from catapults [have] bruised my flesh; again and again I have been struck by stones or clubs—and all for your sakes: for your glory and your gain. Over every land and sea, across river, mountain, and plain I [have] led you to the world's end, a victorious army."
—*Alexander the Great, addressing his troops*

ADDITIONAL RESOURCES

SELECT BIBLIOGRAPHY

De Sélincourt, Aubrey, trans. *Arrian: The Campaigns of Alexander*. New York: Dorset Press, 1986.

Gergel, Tania, ed. *Alexander the Great: The Brief Life and Towering Exploits of History's Greatest Conqueror, as Told by His Original Biographers*. New York: Penguin Books, 2004.

Lane Fox, Robin. *Alexander the Great*. New York: Penguin Books, 2004.

Rogers, Guy MacLean. *Alexander: The Ambiguity of Greatness*. New York: Random House, 2004.

FURTHER READING

Behnke, Alison. *The Conquests of Alexander the Great*. Minneapolis: Twenty-First Century Books, 2008.

Shecter, Vicky Alvear, and Terry Naughton, illus. *Alexander the Great Rocks the World*. Plain City, OH: Darby Creek Publishing, 2006.

Slavicek, Louise Chipley. *Alexander the Great*. Detroit: Lucent Books, 2005.

Web Links

To learn more about Alexander the Great, visit ABDO Publishing Company online at **www.abdopublishing.com**. Web sites about Alexander the Great are featured on our Book Links page. These links are routinely monitored and updated to provide the most current information available.

Places to Visit

The Oriental Institute of the University of Chicago: The Robert and Deborah Aliber Persian Gallery
1155 East Fifty-eighth Street, Chicago, IL 60637
773-702-9520
www.oi.uchicago.edu/museum/persia
The museum exhibit includes approximately 1,000 artifacts from ancient Persian cultures, including ruins of Persepolis.

The University of Pennsylvania Museum of Archaeology and Anthropology: The Greek World
3260 South Street, Philadelphia, PA 19104
215-898-4000
www.museum.upenn.edu/new/exhibits/galleries/greekworld.html
Learn about various aspects of life in ancient Greece in this comprehensive exhibit. On display are 400 artifacts, such as vases, sculptures, and coins, dating from the eleventh century BCE through the first century BCE.

GLOSSARY

assassin
A killer who often secretly plots or uses surprise tactics to murder an important or famous person.

bloodline
Lineage, or one's history of descendants.

cavalry
A unit of the army made up of troops who do battle on horseback.

city-state
An independent, self-governing region typically consisting of a single prominent city and its surrounding territories.

divine
Related to a god or some other supreme power; bearing godlike characteristics.

heir
A ruler who inherits a position of power.

Hellenistic
Referring to the period of Greek civilization and widespread Greek cultural influence following the death of Alexander the Great.

heritage
Cultural traits or traditions that are passed from one generation to the next or that bear some sort of historical significance.

hoplites
Ancient Greek infantry soldiers who typically bore heavy arms into battle.

infantry
A unit of the army made up of foot soldiers.

mercenaries
Soldiers paid to fight for a country other than their own.

mutiny
To openly revolt against an authority figure such as a military commander.

oracle
Either a prophet or a prophecy predicted by someone who sees the future as it is revealed to that person by a god.

pages
Young male attendants who typically serve or defend a nobleman or a person of elevated rank.

phalanx
A military formation that consists of soldiers grouped closely beside each other in rows that run eight to ten men deep.

pillage
To loot, steal, or rob.

regent
An official who rules or maintains order during a monarch's absence.

sarissas
Long, deadly, sharp-tipped spears.

satraps
Governors or local rulers who reigned over provinces in ancient Persia.

siege engines
Machines such as catapults and battering rams that were used in warfare to overcome city walls and other strategic fortifications.

subcontinent
An expansive region or landmass that constitutes a distinctive portion of a larger continent.

talents
Ancient units of mass that were often used to measure gold, silver, or other precious metals involved in monetary dealings.

tribute
Payment that is often contractual and that was frequently used between ancient nations as a sign of respect, allegiance, or submission.

Source Notes

Chapter 1. A Horseman's Skills and a Hint at Greatness

1. Guy MacLean Rogers. *Alexander: The Ambiguity of Greatness*. New York: Random House, 2004. 6.

2. Tania Gergel, ed. *Alexander the Great: The Brief Life and Towering Exploits of History's Greatest Conqueror, as Told by His Original Biographers*. New York: Penguin Books, 2004. 7.

3. Alexander *by Plutarch*. 4 Oct. 2000. Massachusetts Institute of Technology: The Internet Classics Archive. 22 Aug. 2007 <http://classics.mit.edu/Plutarch/alexandr.html>.

4. Guy MacLean Rogers. *Alexander:The Ambiguity of Greatness*. New York: Random House, 2004. 6.

Chapter 2. Raised to Rule an Empire

1. Guy MacLean Rogers. *Alexander: The Ambiguity of Greatness*. New York: Random House, 2004. 5.

2. Tania Gergel, ed. *Alexander the Great: The Brief Life and Towering Exploits of History's Greatest Conqueror, as Told by His Original Biographers*. New York: Penguin Books, 2004. 8.

3. Ibid. 4.

4. Ibid. 3.

5. Ibid. 3.

Chapter 3. The Final Years of a Father and Son

1. Tania Gergel, ed. *Alexander the Great: The Brief Life and Towering Exploits of History's Greatest Conqueror, as Told by His Original Biographers*. New York: Penguin Books, 2004. 9.

2. Ibid. 10.

3. Ibid. 10.

Chapter 4. Early Achievements on Asian Soil

1. Tania Gergel, ed. *Alexander the Great: The Brief Life and Towering Exploits of History's Greatest Conqueror, as Told by His Original Biographers*. New York: Penguin Books, 2004. 31.

2. Ibid. 32.

3. Ibid. 28.

4. Robin Lane Fox. *Alexander the Great*. New York: Penguin Books, 2004. III.

5. Tania Gergel, ed. *Alexander the Great: The Brief Life and Towering Exploits of History's Greatest Conqueror, as Told by His Original Biographers*. New York: Penguin Books, 2004. 44.
6. Peter Green. *Alexander of Macedon, 356–323 B.C.: A Historical Biography*. Berkeley and Los Angeles: University of California Press, 1991. 55.

Chapter 5. A Clash of Kings
1. Aubrey De Sélincourt, trans. *Arrian: The Campaigns of Alexander*. New York: Dorset Press, 1986. 112.
2. Ibid. 112.
3. Tania Gergel, ed. *Alexander the Great: The Brief Life and Towering Exploits of History's Greatest Conqueror, as Told by His Original Biographers*. New York: Penguin Books, 2004. 50.
4. Ibid. 66.

Chapter 6. Intent on Absolute Glory
1. Guy MacLean Rogers. *Alexander: The Ambiguity of Greatness*. New York: Random House, 2004. 101.
2. Ibid. 101.
3. Tania Gergel, ed. *Alexander the Great: The Brief Life and Towering Exploits of History's Greatest Conqueror, as Told by His Original Biographers*. New York: Penguin Books, 2004. 71.
4. Ibid. 74–75.
5. Ibid. 76.

Chapter 7. Bittersweet Successes
1. Tania Gergel, ed. *Alexander the Great: The Brief Life and Towering Exploits of History's Greatest Conqueror, as Told by His Original Biographers*. New York: Penguin Books, 2004. 81.
2. Ibid. 91.
3. Ibid. 82.
4. Guy MacLean Rogers. *Alexander: The Ambiguity of Greatness*. New York: Random House, 2004. 139.
5. Ibid. 177.
6. Ibid. 164.

Source Notes Continued

Chapter 8. Endless Ambition in India

1. Guy MacLean Rogers. *Alexander: The Ambiguity of Greatness*. New York: Random House, 2004. 200.
2. Ibid. 200.
3. Aubrey De Sélincourt, trans. *Arrian: The Campaigns of Alexander*. New York: Dorset Press, 1986. 293.
4. Ibid. 296–297.
5. Ibid. 294.
6. Ibid. 298.
7. Ibid. 319.

Chapter 9. Never Another Like Him

1. Aubrey De Sélincourt, trans. *Arrian: The Campaigns of Alexander*. New York: Dorset Press, 1986. 337.
2. Ibid. 363.
3. Tania Gergel, ed. *Alexander the Great: The Brief Life and Towering Exploits of History's Greatest Conqueror, as Told by His Original Biographers*. New York: Penguin Books, 2004. 136.
4. Guy MacLean Rogers. *Alexander: The Ambiguity of Greatness*. New York: Random House, 2004. 275.
5. Aubrey De Sélincourt, trans. *Arrian: The Campaigns of Alexander*. New York: Dorset Press, 1986. 398.

INDEX

Index Continued

ABOUT THE AUTHOR

Katie Marsico writes children's books from her home near
Chicago, Illinois. She lives with her husband and their two
children. Before beginning her career as an author, Ms. Marsico
worked as a managing editor in children's publishing. She will
probably never travel as extensively or often as Alexander the Great,
but she at least attempts to get as far as the Gulf Coast of Florida on
a yearly basis.

PHOTO CREDITS